EXPERIFAITH
At the Heart of Every Religion
*An Experiential Approach to Individual Spirituality
and Improved Interfaith Relations*

Gudjon Bergmann
www.experifaith.com

To the human family.
Let us remember the things
that bind us together.

CONTENTS

GRATITUDE

No writer can do it all on his own. I want to thank the following people who have supported me, guided me, and inspired me.

My wife, Jóhanna Bóel Bergmann, is at the top of that list. She is my supporter in chief and her continued faith keeps me going.

My deceased father, Guðlaugur Bergmann, and my deceased grandmother, Laufey Torfadóttir, have my deepest gratitude. They both spoke to me openly about religion and spirituality and pointed me in the direction of teachers and books that influenced me profoundly.

My teachers are also deserving of my gratitude, especially Yogi Shanti Desai, who has been my mentor for almost twenty years and was the one who helped me see past dogma and into the experiential realm of spirituality, and the staff at All Faith Seminary, particularly Dr. Rev. Bud James who helped me write this book with encouraging words and insightful feedback.

Lastly, I am grateful to all the authors, teachers, and interfaith thinkers who I have never met but have spurred me forward on this path of inquiry, the most notable of which are Ken Wilber, William James, Aldous Huxley, and Huston Smith.

UNVEILING AN
INTERSPIRITUAL MODEL

"We have, for the first time in history, easy access to all of the world's great religions. Examine the many great traditions — from Christianity to Buddhism, Islam to Taoism, Paganism to Neoplatonism — and you are struck by two items: there are an enormous number of differences between them, and a handful of striking similarities. When you find a few essential items that all, or virtually all, of the world's great religions agree on, you have probably found something incredibly important about the human condition."

Ken Wilber (1949–)
Author and Creator of Integral Theory

In his seminal work, comparative religion author Huston Smith said: "We can define theology as the systematization of thoughts about the symbols that religious experience gives rise to."[1]

His insight reveals a fascinating process. Religious experience gives rise to symbols, symbols give rise to thoughts, and thoughts are then organized into theology. Experience is the starting point; theology is the outcome.

Psychologist William James provided a similar insight. According to him, a prophet who has a religious experience appears to be a lonely madman at first. Then, if his experience-based theology spreads, it is labeled as heresy. Finally, if the doctrine triumphs over persecution, it becomes orthodoxy or tradition.

James notes, however, that once a theology reaches the point of orthodoxy, its days of "inwardness" are over, as orthodoxy effectively stops "all later bubblings of the fountain from which in purer days it drew its own supply of inspiration."[2]

It is quite remarkable when you think about it. Two of the world's most renowned religious thinkers put *experience* at the heart of every religion. Their insights helped me understand why I have always been attracted to the experiential aspects of religion, why I have spent much of my adult life seeking to unveil the essential elements of spirituality.

In my twenty-five year search, I have encountered a variety of mystical, transcendent, and spiritual experiences. My efforts have included taking part in shamanic sweat lodges, bowing my head in Christian prayer, practicing a wide range of yogic

---

[1] Huston Smith, *The World's Religions* (HarperOne, 1958)
[2] William James, *The Varieties of Religious Experience* (Longmans, Green & Co., 1902)

techniques, mentally journeying inward with the aid of New Age visualizations, experiencing deep states of nondual meditation, and contemplating the differences between Eastern and Western philosophy.

My journey has been interesting, to say the least, but it has also been perplexing, mainly because I've encountered the same East-West paradox time and time again. Paths of Eastern origins have been telling me to let go, reconnect with the fabric of my being, be in the moment, and detach from the world of shadows and light. At the same time, my semi-secular Christian upbringing has been urging me to do good, be good, be a force for change, and be invested in the world.

This contradiction has been a consistent pebble in my shoe. Let go or be good? Be in the moment or work for social change? One path emphasizes detachment while the other champions love and good works. For years, I vacillated between the two, never finding a coherent or satisfactory approach that included both.

Then something remarkable happened.

In 2016, I entered All Faiths Seminary to study the world's religions and become an interfaith minister. Soon thereafter, an interspiritual model began to unveil itself to me in fragments. I started seeing a pattern, a link between spiritual paths, clear connections where I had seen none before.

The pattern unveiled itself to me at a faster pace when I let go of the narrative approach to religion — i.e. the stories of who said what to whom and what that means — and focused solely on the experiential approach. I came to understand that while religions are not the same, our abilities to experience are. We all have the same equipment to work with, you see. Each human being has access to a body, emotions, a mind, and all cultures have reported the existence of a spirit or soul of some sort.[3]

Once the model had revealed itself to me, I felt a sense of calm. I could finally think coherently about religion and spirituality. The pebble in my shoe had been removed.

In hindsight, I can't say whether the model came to me or I came to it. However it came into existence, the result is clear. *Experifaith* is an undiluted and inclusive instrument that can be used by both individuals and groups who seek a deeper understanding of the fundamental aspects of faith.

The Notion of Shared Experience

"The distinctive aspect of mysticism is something that cannot be understood by study, but only by dhawq [tasting/immediate experience]. There is a big difference between knowing the meaning and causes of health and satiety, and being healthy and satisfied."

Al-Ghazali (1058–1111)
Persian Philosopher and Muslim Theologian

When I started showing *Experifaith* to others — presenting it on napkins and scraps of paper to friends, family, clergy, mentors and philosophy doctors, to name a few — it soon became evident that the model had potential.

---

[3] The trinity of body, mind, and spirit is one of the few common threads found in all of the world's religions; Ken Wilber, *The Marriage of Sense and Soul* (Broadway Books, 1998)

It resolved a persistent philosophical dilemma between East and West and presented itself as a useful tool for cataloging spiritual experiences and actions, thusly giving people a more complete view of the most intimate aspects of their spiritual life.

More importantly, *Experifaith* showed itself to be a valuable template for a new type of interfaith discussions. Unlike other interfaith approaches — which usually revolve around open-mindedness towards religious stories and customs — the model demonstrated how believers can sincerely practice their faith, record their experiences, and then compare the outcomes with practitioners of different faiths.

This notion of shared experience is important.

A hiker, for example, has much more in common with other hikers who have walked paths foreign to him than with sedentary people who have never hiked anywhere but have read books about the hiker's favorite path.

If someone has hiked several mountains in Switzerland, for instance, he or she is likely to have more in common with those who have hiked in the Rocky Mountains than with those who have never hiked at all. The terrain may be different, but the act of hiking is similar.

The same is true about spirituality. The acts of praying, meditating, fasting, contemplating deeply, and having other direct forms of experience, all influence practitioners differently than mere reading or listening. Moreover, because we all have the same tools to work with — body, mind, and spirit — practitioners from different faiths will have more in common than they realize.

Presenting Experifaith

"As we live, we grow and our beliefs change. They must change. So I think we should live with this constant discovery. We should be open to this adventure in heightened awareness of living. We should stake our whole existence on our willingness to explore and experience."

Martin Buber (1878–1965)
Austrian-born Israeli Jewish Philosopher

The *Experifaith* model is composed of seven elements; two experiential paths, the principle of their separation and connection, and four spiritual actions, all of which I will explain on the following pages.

In regards to how the model is presented, one of my favorite quotes about writing comes from mathematician, inventor, and Christian philosopher Blaise Pascal, who said: "This letter would be shorter if I'd had more time."[4]

Thankfully, I did have plenty of time to write this book and opted for brevity and clarity.

Explanations are concise. Examples are clear and to the point. The book reads like a visit to a French restaurant, with small portions that provide plenty of flavors.

Admittedly, *Experifaith* has its limitations. It is not meant to teach about specific religions, answer theological questions, excuse intolerant religious behaviors, or solve racial, cultural or religious con-

---

[4] This quote has also been attributed to John Locke, Benjamin Franklin, Henry David Thoreau and Woodrow Wilson, but as far as I can tell, Pascal was the one who phrased it originally.

flicts, most of which are historical and geopolitical in nature. Nor is it meant to convert anyone or challenge religious convictions. You can be safe in the assumption that your religion, faith, or spiritual path, will be respected throughout. As the name suggests, the focus is on interrelated experiences, not on the finer points of theology.

My hope is that the *Experifaith* model will cause believers and seekers alike to think deeply about their approach to faith and spirituality, and further encourage them to practice and reflect on how their experiences relate to other religions and spiritual paths. Moreover, it is my sincere wish that the model be used — along with other approaches — to facilitate lively and enlightening interfaith conversations.

Gudjon Bergmann, 2017
www.experifaith.com

THE TWO PATHS OF
EXPERIENTIAL FAITH

"The splendor of the rose and the whiteness of the lily do not rob the little violet of its scent nor the daisy of its simple charm. If every tiny flower wanted to be a rose, spring would lose its loveliness."

Saint Thérèse de Lisieux (1873–1897)
Roman Catholic French Carmelite Nun.

When studying the world's religions, there appear to be two primary paths available to those who want to practice their faith.

One path is internal and contemplative in nature. The other is emotional, external, and actionable in nature. I have identified these as the paths of *oneness* and *goodness*.

Although both exist in all of the major religions—Islam has Sufism, Christianity has Mysticism, Hinduism has Yoga, Judaism has Kabbalah, various forms of Buddhism differ from internal to external, and so on—it is fair to say that the East has favored the internal path of oneness while the West—especially the Abrahamic traditions, including Judaism, Christianity, and Islam—has focused more on the external path of goodness. Understanding the difference between the two is vital.

Oneness is nondual in nature, based on the concept that there is only one entity underlying all reality. Oneness encompasses practices such as meditation, contemplative prayer, fasting, silence, and retreat.

Goodness, on the other hand, is dual in nature and cannot exist in a vacuum. Goodness encompasses practices such as love, service, prayers of gratitude, prayers of surrender, prayers of petition, forgiveness, tolerance, and compassion.

To get a more comprehensive view, let us explore these two experiential paths separately.

For the purpose of clarity, both of them will be presented as circles, oneness with an internal direction and goodness with an external direction.

The Path of Goodness

"Do all the good you can. By all the means you can. In all the ways you can. In all the places you can. At all the times you can. To all the people you can. As long as ever you can."

John Wesley (1703–1791)
Anglican Cleric and Founder of Methodism

Every religion offers a version of love thy neighbor as thyself or the golden rule.[5] Devotees who follow the path of goodness are encouraged to be loving, compassionate, selfless, forgiving and, above all, good.

The golden rule is a positive message. Just imagine if each person truly loved his or her innermost being, altruistically. That person could not help but love and care for others. One could easily envision a peace-loving society if everyone's cup of inner love were overflowing.

If only it were that easy.

The problem is that human beings are notoriously difficult to love. Our bodies have needs that remind us of animal behavior, and we don't have to look very far to find greed, jealousy, hatred, sexual aggression, and violence—even within ourselves. On top of that, our emotions are messy and our minds irrational.

The naked ape is not very lovable, at least, not at first glance.

When we take a deeper look, however, we find the potential for grace, compassion, love, and all the other virtues of goodness.

This sentiment of seeing potential in humans has been reflected time and time again in popular culture. Nearly every movie about aliens, who are about to destroy the human race but decide against it, includes the sentence: "But, there is good in them."

With all of that taken into account, we see that human love is a complicated and potentially chaotic phenomenon. Telling people to love themselves,

---

[5] Rev. Jon Mundy Ph.D., *What is Mysticism?* (Royal Fireworks Press, 2008)

and, furthermore, to love their neighbors, is a tall order.

Religions vary in their approach when it comes to recipes for cultivating love.

Some traditions offer a psychological approach, teaching tolerance, compassion, and forgiveness towards oneself in order to be able to extend the same to others, or vice versa, loving others to find love for oneself.

Others approach the task by claiming that love is divine in nature and, therefore, one should surrender human tendencies — especially destructive ones — and focus on allowing love to flow through oneself rather than try to create a well within.

The interfaith perspective says that there is probably truth to both of these and several other approaches.

Expanding the Circle of Goodness

"There's a light seed grain inside,
You fill it with yourself or it dies"

Rumi (1207–1273)
Persian Poet, Islamic Scholar, and Sufi Mystic
Translated by Coleman Barks

Let us assume, for the moment, that you wish to love thy neighbor as thyself. You would first use whatever method of increasing love that your religion or spiritual path prescribes, and then try to expand that love.

The following diagram illustrates the process of expansion.

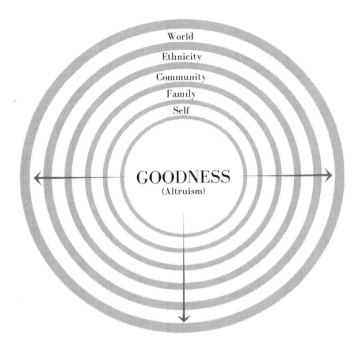

Now, ask yourself. Who are you willing to show goodness to and why? Where do you draw the line? At your family, your community, your country, other religions, other ethnicities? Where does your ability to extend goodness dissipate? Is there a difference between your ability to perform good actions and your ability to extend good thoughts? What is your measuring stick for goodness?

Before we continue, I want you to understand that this diagram is in no way meant to shame anyone. Energy is limited, and those who work on expanding their circle of goodness typically make great sacrifices.[6] If you are able to show goodness to yourself, your family, friends, and maybe to some in your community, you are doing better than most. In fact, it can be harder to show goodness to those who stand close to you than to those who are in faraway places. If more people tended to their own gardens, all of society would flourish as a result.

Expanding the circle of goodness is a process of establishing, transcending, and then including. For example, one can establish love for oneself — not the selfish kind, but the caring kind — then transcend (expand) that love, and establish love for another person while at the same time including love for oneself.

As noted above, this becomes harder as the circle enlarges because there is always some kind of letting go or sacrifice involved.

Becoming a parent is a great example. Parents must give up many of their old and often selfish ways to tend to their young ones, which makes the act of sacrificing for another human being the oldest form of love and goodness. Yet, many fail because they are not willing to endure the costs involved.

Great servants of humanity have known this. Take the example of Mahatma Gandhi. His circle of goodness began with his family, expanded to include the Indian people in South Africa, widened further to include the Indian people in India, and in his final days, he was working for goodness in the

---

[6] The word *sacrifice* is used here—and for the remainder of the book—in the dictionary meaning; to give up (something important or valued) for the sake of other considerations.

entire world. One might even say that the example of his life is still working for global goodness. However, as Gandhi progressed and expanded his circle of goodness, he made sacrifices. The time he spent on the road or in prison for a worthy cause took away time that he spent with his family, and some of his children suffered as a result. One, in particular, became an alcoholic and largely blamed his father for the situation. Nevertheless, Gandhi never sacrificed his spiritual practice. He believed that without a source of energy he would not be able to keep expanding his mission of peace, love, and unity.

Another example is Mother Teresa — or Saint Teresa of Calcutta, as she is now known — who sacrificed many things, including the ability to have a family of her own, in order to take care of the sick, poor and dying. Still, in the same way as Gandhi did, she never sacrificed the time she spent in prayer.

A number of the world's religions take the long view when it comes to the expansion of goodness. They instruct people to help moderately with donations of time and money during their working years but then encourage increased community involvement as time passes, with the knowledge that it is easier to help and serve when people are operating from a surplus and the kids are out of the house.

There are, however, always a chosen few who select a life of service and asceticism at a young age, sacrificing what one would consider a normal life for the privilege of serving a higher power and the community as a whole.

Goodness Cannot Exist in a Vacuum

"To wish to act like angels while we are still in this world is nothing but folly."

Saint Teresa of Avila (1515–1582)
Carmelite Nun, Spanish Mystic, and Catholic Saint

For goodness to exist, there has to be an opposite or contrast of some kind. We cannot know what is good unless we also know its antithesis. To see white, we need black. To see light, we need darkness. This is the central truth of duality.

Furthermore, because there is a correlation between a strong attraction toward one thing and a strong repulsion to its opposite, there exist two very different approaches to the cultivation of goodness.

One is the nurturing of goodness itself, including the intentional development of love, compassion, forgiveness, and tolerance. We can call this the hopeful and positive approach.

The other is to reject everything that is not considered good, which has been thusly labeled by clergy, scriptures, or a community of believers, sometimes even going so far as trying to dispel it from the world. We can call this the vigilant and critical approach.

In every religion, both forces exist. One is forever optimistic; the other forever cautious. One believes that there is nothing but good in people; the other believes that we must resist destructive urges from both within and without.[7]

---

[7] For those who believe in nothing but the good, it must be noted that anthropologists have yet to find the remnants of a culture that

As before, the interfaith perspective acknowledges that there is probably truth to both and warns against extremes.

Perfectionism and Harsh Judgment

"Compassion is not a popular virtue. Very often when I talk to religious people, and mention how important it is that compassion is the key, that it's the sine-qua-non of religion, people look kind of balked, and stubborn sometimes, as much to say, what's the point of having religion if you can't disapprove of other people?"

Karen Armstrong (1944–)
Former Roman Catholic Sister and Author

The potential downside of goodness as a primary spiritual path tends to be *perfectionism*, a trait often coupled with harsh judgment. In every human era there have been those who have striven for perfection, and, in every era, most, if not all, have failed. It seems that perfection is not built into the human system.

A simple formula exists to guard against perfectionism. It consists of *humility* and *humor*. Humility reminds us that we don't have all the answers, no matter how much we think we know, and, therefore, we should not judge others too harshly. Without humility we may begin to believe that our way is the only way, going so far as to force our beliefs on others. Humor, on the other hand, prompts us not to take ourselves too seriously. For example, lack of humor is an indicative sign

---

functioned on the basis of absolute social permissiveness; Huston Smith, *The World's Religions* (HarperOne, 1958)

of religious cult behavior[8] and we don't want that, do we? A healthy sense of humor allows us to laugh at our shortcomings, especially when we are having difficulties following the most pious of religious prescriptions.

It may be hard for us to accept, but nobody is perfect. We would be wise to adopt some of the most insightful spiritual advice written in the 20th Century and "claim spiritual progress rather than spiritual perfection."[9]

The Goodness Question

"If one is cruel to himself, how can we expect him to be compassionate with others?"

Hasdai ibn Shaprut (915–970)
Jewish Scholar, Physician, and Patron of Science

At the end of the day, developing goodness comes down to a simple question: *Will this emotion, thought or action, increase or decrease my capacity for goodness?*

If it increases my capacity for goodness, then I am on the right track. If it decreases my capacity, then I need to recalibrate the course I have chosen.

Simple? Yes.

Easy to do? No.

That is why it's called a spiritual *practice*.

---

[8] According to research by Dr. Arthur Deikman
[9] *The Big Book of AA* (Alcoholic Anonymous World Services, 1939)

The Path of Oneness

"In the beginning was only being, one without a second. Out of himself he brought forth the cosmos and entered into everything in it. There is nothing that does not come from him. Of everything he is the inmost Self. He is the truth; he is the Self supreme. You are that."

Chandogya Upanishad
An ancient Vedanta treatise
Translated by Eknath Easwaran

The second of the two experiential religious paths is contemplative in nature and consists of introspection, meditation, observation, and copious amounts of silence.

Due to the extroverted nature of most humans, the path of oneness has historically not been a popular one. In fact, in most religious traditions spiritual practices of oneness are not offered as options until the practitioner in question has had enough of the world. The approach has usually been reserved for those willing to give up all worldly belongings to become ascetics, monks, or nuns.

The path of oneness is considered exceptionally difficult, both from intellectual and practical standpoints. Whether the practice is called Yoga, Sufism, Kabbalah, Taoism, Christian Mysticism, Buddhism, or something else, it involves a lot of training and deep contemplation about the nature of the world. It is not for everyone, nor should it be.

Over the centuries, only a few have truly mastered the path of oneness[10], but their insights into the nature of the world, including mind, body, and

---

[10] Ken Wilber, *Kosmic Consciousness* (Sounds True, 2003)

spirit, have been nothing short of amazing.

Fortunately, every religion has had their share of mystics, which means that today everyone is afforded the opportunity to study oneness from within their religion or spiritual path—if they are so inclined.

For the purpose of clarity, consider the following diagram.

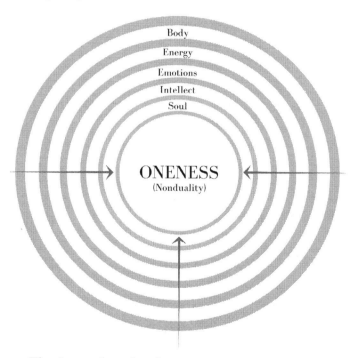

The inward path of oneness seems to be one of exploration, detachment, and embodiment.

The practitioner studies the nature of the body, life energy, emotions, intellect, and so on—even masters some of those elements along the way—and then detaches from the veils that do not meet the criterion of oneness, which is that oneness must be *unchanging*. If it changes, then it is not the eternal essence, not the underlying reality, not oneness.

The master is then said to embody mind, emotions, energy, and matter, from the standpoint of oneness—a state often called enlightenment.

Studying the history of spirituality in the West, it is interesting to see that many learned men, including physicists, doctors, and writers, were attracted to this type of spirituality in the early part of the 20th Century. The ancient philosophies of oneness rhymed with the emerging worldview that physics had produced at the time, which claimed that energy and consciousness were at the core of everything in our dualistic world, that everything was connected at the most basic level. For a moment in time, Eastern mysticism merged with Western scientific thinking.

Today, however, many people use practical techniques devised by devotees of the oneness path. In the later parts of the 20th Century and early parts of the 21st Century, we saw a resurgence in oneness practices in relation to stress management and living in the moment. Peace of mind became a coveted prize for those who wished to turn their backs on a chaotic and stressful external world.

Many have benefitted from using these techniques—including myself and the people who have attended my yoga, meditation, and stress management seminars over the years—but few have embraced the entirety of oneness philosophies due to their inherent difficulty and apparent discord with the goodness path; the latter being one of the main reasons why I wrote this book.

Promises and Perils

"Remain in the world, act in the world, do whatsoever is needful, and yet remain transcendental, aloof, detached, a lotus flower in the pond."

Osho (1931–1990)
Mystic and Spiritual Teacher

Inner peace is the central promise of the oneness path. According to the oneness traditions, once a practitioner knows oneness firsthand — in the same way that he or she would experientially know the taste of chocolate, the feel of the sun, the refreshing nature of water, or the tender sensation of a loving kiss — then fear of death — which is known to spiritual practitioners as the root of all other fears — will drop away.

Those who have repeatedly experienced such states of oneness are reported to show unparalleled equanimity. For them, there is no high or low, up or down, good or bad. There is only this, only now, only oneness.

The potential downsides related to oneness practices are *apathy* and *mistaken identification*. One is based on detachment without embodiment, the other on inaccurate attachment.

Apathy takes hold when the practice of detachment leads a practitioner to think that nothing is of importance, that nothing is better or worse, that it's all a dream, all a mirage. This is detachment without embodiment.

An example would be a driver who thought he was the car he was driving. If he realized that he and the car were, in fact, separate, then that would be a great discovery (detachment).

However, after the discovery was made he would need to continue driving the car (embodiment) otherwise the results might be disastrous — in his case a car crash, in the spiritual aspirant's case apathy and sometimes depression.

Historically, most meditation practitioners have been taught to counteract this tendency with hours upon hours of service. They have been instructed to perform benevolent physical activities to stay grounded.

The two practices — of meditation on one hand and service on the other — appear to balance each other out and keep practitioners from succumbing to apathy.

Mistaken identification is another potential pitfall on the oneness path. Here, the practitioner may start to identify with the practices rather than the goal, thusly making the means equal to the end.

Using driving as a metaphor again, the driver could start obsessing over his driving skills, the appearance of his car, or the fuel he chooses for it, rather than focusing on where he is going.

When mistaken identification happens on the spiritual path, breathing techniques and physical exercises — which are important in their own right — or emotional visualizations and healing practices — which can serve as stepping-stones if used effectively — can replace the end goal of unveiling oneness. The practitioner attaches himself to the tools and forgets that he or she is working towards a particular outcome.[11] The historical cure for this

---

[11] If the ultimate goal is not to unveil oneness, then there is no harm in making the techniques—everything from yoga exercises to mindfulness—into the primary goal. However, if the ultimate goal

has been to keep the ultimate goal in mind at all times.

The Oneness Question

"I laugh when I hear that the fish
in the water is thirsty.
You wander restlessly from forest
to forest while the Reality
is within your own dwelling."

Kabir (1440–1518)
Poet, Indian Mystic, and Saint

Oneness practices revolve around noticing whether you are creating or removing obstacles as you attempt to unveil the underlying reality.

People on the oneness path repeatedly ask a simple question: *Does this action, emotion or thought, help or hinder my attempts to unveil oneness?*

The path involves persistent efforts to unveil that which does not change.

---

becomes oneness at any point, then it is important to move the goal post.

THE PRINCIPLE OF CONNECTION AND SEPARATION

"Philosophy is the account which the human mind gives to itself of the constitution of the world. Two cardinal facts lie forever at the base; the one, and the two. — 1. Unity, or Identity; and, 2. Variety. We unite all things by perceiving the law which pervades them; by perceiving the superficial differences and the profound resemblances. But every mental act, — this very perception of identity or oneness, recognizes the difference of things. Oneness and otherness. It is impossible to speak or to think without embracing both."

Ralph Waldo Emerson (1803–1882)
American Essayist and Transcendentalist

Devotees of these two spiritual paths of experience—oneness and goodness—have been at odds for centuries.

Proponents of the oneness path have insisted that the goal of spirituality is to reconnect with everlasting eternity. They yearn to taste the quintessence of their being, to transcend time and space, to be unified with *the one*.

In the other camp, advocates of the goodness path have traditionally seen stark choices in the world. They believe we should choose love, compassion, beauty, truth, and altruism over hatred, fear, anger, judgment, and other opposites of goodness. To them, there are constructive forces in the world that are being challenged by destructive ones. Their goal has been to stand their ground and choose to be good above all else.

Even with those apparent differences, both paths have found homes within each of the world's religions. As noted earlier, Hinduism offers the oneness path of Yoga, Judaism offers Kabbalah, Islam offers Sufism, Christianity offers Mysticism, and so on. Whatever the arrangement, the two paths have historically found ways to co-exist.

Co-existence, however, does not mean that the two paths are the same. Over the centuries there have been numerous attempts to merge the two, for example, by saying that there is only oneness and that oneness is good.

These attempts have all failed because they have run into the same theological dilemma. Oneness is nondual in nature, as in, there is only one, while goodness is dual in nature because for it to exist there must be something other than good.

If oneness is the coin, goodness is one side of the coin; if oneness is the ocean, goodness is a set of benign waves; if oneness is the entire color spectrum, goodness is represented by bright and beautiful colors. It is impossible to reduce the coin to one side, the ocean to a set of waves, or the color spectrum to only bright and beautiful colors. Oneness is all that is. Goodness is a choice between two or more things; between yin and yang, heaven and hell, high and low, good and bad... the list is never ending.

Attempts to unify or merge the two are forever fraught with this philosophical inconsistency. How can oneness be everything when it can be reduced to less than that? It is much more consistent to see the two paths as connected but separate.

Connected Through Eternal Flow

"Spiders can't help making flytraps, and men can't help making symbols. That's what the human brain is there for — to turn the chaos of given experience into a set of manageable symbols."

Aldous Huxley (1894–1963)
Author and Philosopher

The dualistic world, which contains goodness, is created out of oneness. From then on, the flow is never ending from oneness into goodness and back again. The paths are simultaneously connected and separate.

This realization creates an important understanding, both within religions and between religions. It clearly shows why the values of goodness cannot be debated against the values of oneness.

Oneness is the essence of everything, and therefore it has no specific values aside from unity.

Goodness, on the other hand, is all about values. Goodness means that it is better to [fill in the blank] than to [fill in the blank].

Once we acknowledge both their connectedness and their separateness, the paths are able to co-exist. We can stop debating the merits of one based on the merits of the other. Goodness must be practiced, debated and appreciated on the merits of goodness, and oneness must be practiced, debated and appreciated on its own merits.

Seeing both the separation and connection means that we don't have to make one side wrong and the other one right. In fact, both sides are right within their own realm of thought and contemplation.

Those who try to unveil oneness are correct in their approach. Their primary goals are peace of mind and unity.

Those who emphasize good thoughts and deeds in this world are also right. Their primary goals are developing love, cultivating relationships, and worshipping the divine.

And those who attempt to practice both paths can do so only when they accept this theological oxymoron and stop trying to mix oil with water.

The bottom line is that both paths have historically found a way to exist side-by-side in the world's religions. We should respect them as such.

THE FOUR ACTIONS OF EXPERIENTIAL FAITH

"Religion is doing; a man does not merely think his religion or feel it, he 'lives' his religion as much as he is able, otherwise it is not religion but fantasy or philosophy. Whether he likes it or not he shows his attitude towards religion by his actions and he can show his attitude only by his actions. Therefore if his actions are opposed to those which are demanded by a given religion he cannot assert that he belongs to that religion."

G.I. Gurdjieff (1866–1949)
Mystic, Philosopher, and Spiritual Teacher

The last four elements in the *Experifaith* model are spiritual actions that are widely practiced in most religious communities around the world. They are, *experimentation, contemplation, love,* and *service*.

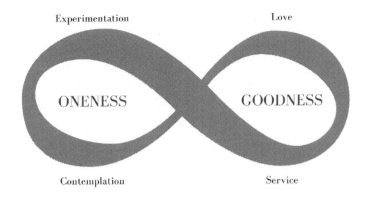

Experimentation   Love

ONENESS   GOODNESS

Contemplation   Service

All four represent viable spiritual activities in their own right, but, historically, experimentation and contemplation have been more closely related to the oneness path while love and service have been staples of the goodness path. However, the four actions are equally available to both, meaning that a person on the goodness path can be drawn to contemplation while a person on the oneness path can be drawn to love and so on. By taking these four groups of actions into account, the *Experifaith* model makes it easier for practitioners to flesh out their chosen path in more detail.

Experimentation

"Mysticism is the most scientific form of religion, for it bases itself, as does all science, on experience and experiment — experiment being only a specialized form of experience, devised either to discover or to verify."

Annie Besant (1847–1933)
British Theosophist

Experimentation is at the heart of the experiential approach to religion. The paths of Sufism, Kabbalah, Yoga, Christian Mysticism, Taoism, and Buddhism all encourage practitioners to experiment with spiritual practices.

When compared to the scientific method, the experimental approach to spirituality is almost identical.

There is a hypothesis (faith, belief, dogma), an experiment (meditation, prayer, fasting, dancing, etc.), followed by a discussion among peers[12] (peer review) and then a conclusion. In best-case scenarios, experiments that produce similar outcomes for most of the practitioners are introduced into the faith community as theologically sound.

Experimental spiritual practices differ in their degree of difficulty. Some are simple, like learning to blow bubbles, while others are infinitely more challenging, like learning how to be a concert pianist, which is a discipline that takes a minimum of eight hours of practice per day.

Short-lived experiences can produce temporary insights (seeing the light, for example), while repeated experiences can become permanent traits (as in, the cultivation of unshakable equanimity).

Each person has to decide whether the proposed benefits outweigh the costs involved.

The most common experiments are meditation, prayer, rituals, and fasting, variations of which have survived the peer review gauntlet in the world's religions time and time again. You will

---

[12] Discussions are confined to those who have put in the same number of hours or similar effort with the same kind of practices, in the same way that complex math discussions are confined to mathematicians with experience of working on the theorems being discussed.

probably find versions of each in your faith tradition.

If you are already engaged in any of these or other spiritual experiments, I encourage you to record your findings, both for personal reflection and comparison with people in your faith community or the larger interfaith community.

However, if you are not practicing anything at the moment but wish to get started, approach the task with an open mind. Take a look at the experiential paths within your tradition and talk to practitioners. If no practitioners are available in your community, read books by those who have walked the path before you. Each religion offers a variety of practices, which means that you should be able to find a practice within your tradition that suits your aspirations.

The upside of approaching spiritual practices like an experiment is that there can be no failure, only different outcomes. Whatever happens, you will learn about yourself and your relationship with the divine along the way.

Contemplation

"Many good sayings are to be found in holy books, but merely reading them will not make one religious."

Ramakrishna (1836–1886)
Indian Yogi and Mystic

At one time in history, theologians and philosophers occupied the same mental space, namely the contemplation of existential topics, such as the nature of the universe, the nature of God, and the meaning of life.

Back then, contemplation was a valid form of personal faith, but over the years it has suffered. The emotional plea of 'get out of your head and into your heart' became the preferred approach in many spiritual and religious circles. Emotion became the alpha and omega, especially in America.[13]

This change resulted in limited choices for intellectual adherents, many of whom abandoned faith altogether. Nonetheless, contemplation still exists as a valid spiritual discipline. Granted, it is harder to contemplate the purpose of life, the nature of spirit and your personal relationship with the divine than it is to pray fervently — it may even create a headache or two — but for people who feel the need for both spirituality and intellectual stimulation, contemplation may be the most appropriate spiritual activity.

Contemplation can take many forms. It can transpire in silence and isolation, take place among peers or in study groups, or occur as an internal reaction to reading scripture. In that context, we need to briefly revisit the topic of narrative religion or storyfaith.

For many, stories represent the very core of their religion, and yet, for a number of reasons, such as potential divisiveness and different interpretations, I set the narrative approach aside while I was in the process of unveiling the *Experifaith* model. The universality of the model is not based on comparisons between religious stories but rather on the similarity between human experiences.

Yet, the question remains. How should one app-

---

[13] Stephen Prothero, *Religious Literacy* (HarperOne, 2008)

roach religious stories on the contemplative path? The answer is, experientially. Read the stories, not with an extreme attitude, either to dismiss them all as nonsense or accept them all as absolute truth, but to compare them to your own life.

Joseph Campbell, a great scholar of myth, was adamant in his view that there is value in all of the stories that humans have told each other over the ages, especially myths and parables. When you allow yourself to reflect and contemplate, to compare religious stories to your own life, especially to your thoughts, feelings and actions, you can be sure to deepen your understanding of the human-divine connection and reveal unexpected insights.

Read and compare. Read and reflect.

That is the experiential approach.

In the contemplative paradigm, creating a group where spiritual thought is stimulated can be of great significance. Most thinking is typically done in private, during periods of silence, writing, or reading. However, the ability to air thoughts and have them mirrored back, having the opportunity to listen to the inner workings of other minds who share your passion for contemplation, can add layers of meaning to your spiritual life that are difficult to attain in other ways. I have belonged to many such groups over the years and have always gained from the interactions.

To recap, contemplation is the act of looking for spiritual insights rather than factual knowledge.

The practice can extract meaning from the mundane, elicit a deeper understanding of life and the universe, and cause profound personal break-throughs.

Love

"Lord, make me an instrument of thy peace.
Where there is hatred, let me sow love,
Where there is injury, pardon;
Where there is doubt, faith;
Where there is despair, hope;
Where there is darkness, light;
And where there is sadness, joy."

St. Francis of Assisi (1182–1226)
Italian Roman Catholic Friar and Preacher

Love is the most complex of all human phenomena. It exists on a spectrum from tolerance and kindness to romantic love and self-sacrifice, reaching its pinnacle in altruism, a love that needs nothing in return.

Although love may be a feeling, cultivating and maintaining it are undeniable actions, and that is where experiential faith steps in, at the level of action.

The world's religions prescribe different methods. Some encourage practitioners to love their enemy as they would themselves, others prescribe the method of lifting the veil and seeing God everywhere, and yet others urge devotees to become vessels of divine love.

Whatever the method, those who see love as an important aspect of religious life allow it to spring them into action—even when the feeling is absent. Caring for a child is a good example. The parent may not feel loving at all times but still performs loving and caring actions.

Those, who follow the path of goodness, often see love as the central aspect of their life. Their entire existence revolves around being heart-centered, loving and good. To them, everything begins and ends at the heart level. They may even encourage others 'not to think too much' and say things like 'it's all about love.'

However, it is important not put one of the four spiritual actions above another. All four are valid in their own right. This release of comparison can also be seen as an expression of love.

While the emotion of love may be difficult to define, the religions of the world seem to agree on one thing. Love becomes more spiritual when it shifts from being selfish to being unselfish.

Service

"God wants us to have soft hearts and hard feet. The trouble with so many of us is that we have hard hearts and soft feet."

Jackie Pullinger (1944–)
Christian Missionary

Service is celebrated as a virtue by all the major religions. The reasons for encouraging the act may differ — service can be a duty, spring from love, stave off the danger of apathy, or be the full expression of goodness — but the end results are similar, with only slight variations. The faithful are always encouraged to serve.

Of the four actions in the *Experifaith* model, service is the most visible. It is easy to measure but hard to do because it demands the unselfish use of time and energy. While it is true that the other three actions — experimentation, contemplation, and the cultivation of love — are practices that also take time, they are part of a personal spiritual path. On the face of it, service does not meet that standard. It doesn't seem to *do* anything for the person who is serving. Nevertheless, those who have made service one of their primary spiritual activities have sworn by the transformative nature of the practice. Reports vary from "it made me understand human unity at a deeper level" to the more self-centered "it helped me get out of my own problems."

Whatever the primary reason, serving others is sown into the fabric of religious life. It is almost impossible to find a place of worship that does not offer a service opportunity of some sort.

THE SEVEN ELEMENTS
OF EXPERIFAITH

"If you look inward, a different dimension opens up. Now instead of things getting more complex, you get to clarity."

Sadhguru Jaggi Vasudev (1957–)
Indian Yogi, Mystic, and Author

Let us briefly review the *Experifaith* model. Here are the seven elements we have covered thus far.

The Oneness Path
The Goodness Path
The Principle of Connection and Separation
The Act of Experimentation
The Act of Contemplation
The Act of Love
The Act of Service

The first two elements, the paths of *oneness* and

goodness, clearly outline the different approaches that have historically been available to religious adherents.

The path of oneness is one of contemplation and introspection. The upside is unity while the potential downsides are apathy and mistaken identification. Practitioners continually remind themselves by asking the question: *Will this help me unveil oneness?*

The path of goodness is one of love and service. The upside is altruism while the potential downsides are perfectionism coupled with harsh judgment. Practitioners continually remind themselves by asking the question: *Will this increase my capacity for goodness?*

One could say that those who value relationships, empathy, forgiveness, love, compassion, and kindness, are more likely to choose the goodness path, while those who want to unveil their essence, merge with the infinite, be in the present moment, or find peace of mind, are more likely to take the road less traveled, the oneness path.

The third element is a principle that shows how the two paths are *connected but separate.* It shows how oneness is all-inclusive and can never be diminished to a part of the dualistic world. Goodness, on the other hand, is an essential part of the dualistic world. It does not exist in a vacuum because it needs a counterpart for contrast.

The infinity symbol is used to illustrate the principle of connection and separation, showing how oneness flows into goodness and goodness back into oneness, creating an eternal current. The reason for making the distinction is that oneness should never be judged by the values of goodness, nor should goodness be judged by the values of oneness. The two exist side-by-side.

The last four elements are the major actions or practices found within all the major religions of the world. *Experimentation* relates to personal practices and rituals, everything from prayer and baptism to meditation and breathing techniques. *Contemplation* is the act of thinking deeply, conversing and reflecting, and can be done in groups or individually. *Love* is the act of cultivating unselfishness and allowing it to spring into action. *Service* is the outward expression of faith, love, and unity. All four are valuable in their own right.

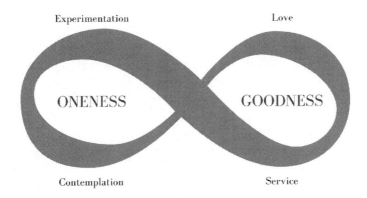

Experimentation — Love

ONENESS — GOODNESS

Contemplation — Service

Where is the Faith in *Experifaith*?

"Take the first step in faith. You don't have to see the whole staircase. Just take the first step."

Martin Luther King Jr. (1929–1968)
Baptist Minister and Civil Rights Leader

Aldous Huxley, who was both an influential novelist and philosopher, distinguished between four meanings of the word faith.

His first definition was faith as *trust*, for example, when we say we have faith in a particular person, system, or product brand.

His second definition was similar to his first, as in, when the word faith is used to describe a *belief in authority*, especially when a person has special qualifications.

Huxley defined the third as our inclination to believe certain propositions that we have not had occasion to verify for ourselves, but which "we *could verify* if we had the inclination, the opportunity, and the necessary capacities."

His fourth definition was synonymous with what some call religious faith, namely a belief in ideas that we *cannot possibly verify*, even if we wanted to. [14]

Reflecting on these four definitions, you can see that the *Experifaith* model does not effectively deal with unverifiable faith — not because dogma and orthodoxy are unimportant, but because they belong to the narrative aspect of religion, which was intentionally left out of the model — nor is anyone being asked to trust based on mere authority.

No, the kind of faith that has been detailed throughout this book fits Huxley's third definition; a faith that a person can verify through experience if he or she has the "inclination, opportunity, and necessary capacities."

This means that the faith aspect of *Experifaith* is encouraging. It proposes that you take experiential elements from your faith tradition, put them into

---

[14] Aldous Huxley, *Perennial Philosophy* (Harper Collins, 1944)

practice, and continue with that practice until you get results. The process of experiential verification can be applied much more widely than most people realize. Yes, it is true that certain elements of religion require faith without corroboration, but there are many more that are verifiable if one is willing to put in the time and effort required.

This does not diminish the concept of faith. No, faith is still faith even when it has the potential to be verified. We can have faith in those who have walked the path before us, faith in the experiential wisdom of a particular spiritual tradition, and faith in the prescribed methods that will help us reach a desirable outcome. It may be different from unverifiable faith, but it is faith nonetheless; a faith that propels us to act.

CREATING YOUR PERSONAL
EXPERIFAITH PORTRAIT

"There is one inevitable criterion of judgment touching religious faith in doctrinal matters. Can you reduce it to practice? If not, have none of it."

Hosea Ballou (1771–1852)
Universalist Clergyman and Theological Writer

This philosophy can now be put into practice by taking the model and using it to create an individualized *Experifaith* portrait. Such a portrait is an experiential representation of a person's predominant spiritual path and the actions that he or she engages in on a regular basis. Creating a personal portrait is a two-step process that will provide you with an intimate representation of your spiritual life.

During the process of creating your personal portrait, it is important to be honest and only write what you currently practice. Filling in the portrait is a way to catalog what you consistently do. The portrait provides you with a summary that allows you to easily understand your personal practices and compare your experiences with others.

The goal is not to find a balance between all the elements, but rather to be true to your choices, tendencies, and faith tradition. Some people are attracted to both paths and all four actions, while others see one action as their primary spiritual purpose. Right or wrong are unhelpful labels in the interfaith context, which means that while you are creating your *Experifaith* portrait, there are no right or wrong answers, only honest or dishonest ones.

Step 1) Oneness or Goodness?

Begin by choosing between the paths of oneness and goodness. The most straightforward way to distinguish between the two is to look at your primary spiritual goals in life.

If your primary goals have an opposite, such as wanting to be good (the opposite of which is bad), hopeful (the opposite of which is apathetic/ pessimistic), or loving (the opposite of which is hateful/fearful), then your path is likely goodness.

However, if your primary spiritual goals do not have an opposite, for example, wanting to be in the eternal now, unveiling peace of mind, achieving the cessation of the thought waves in the mind, or finding unity, then your path is likely oneness.

If you don't want the choice to be binary, you can represent it in percentages, for example, 74% goodness, 26% oneness.

Step 2) List of Actions

The second step is to list all the spiritual or faith-based activities you are currently engaged in. Under the following four headings, you will find suggestions to jump-start the process.

Experimentation: List experimental activities you engage in on a regular basis, such as meditation, prayer, fasting, communion, and other rituals. Try to be as specific as you can, for instance, by listing the types of prayers you practice and whether they are ones of surrender, petition, gratitude or something else; or by describing whether your meditation techniques are based on religious or secular approaches.

Contemplation: List books or passages you read regularly, theological conversations you engage in, contemplative groups you belong to, reflective writing you do, time you spend in deep thought on your own, and other relevant activities.

Love: List actions for maintaining and expanding your love energy, such as the acts of loving, laughing, and forgiving, or showing empathy, tolerance, and compassion, all of which fall somewhere on the love spectrum.

Going to your place of worship, listening to inspirational music, chanting, showing kindness to strangers, sacrificing some of your personal needs for loved ones, and heart-centered meditations can also fall into this category if those activities elevate your feelings of love and devotion.

Service: List everything that you do to help other people, from the home and outward, everything that is based on the unselfish desire to support, encourage, assist, or care for others.

The Parable of the Soup

"Those who recite many scriptures but fail to practice their teachings are like a cowherd counting another's cows. They do not share in the joys of the spiritual life."

The Dhammapada,
Collection of Sayings of the Buddha, Verse 19
Translated by Eknath Easwaran

The parable of the soup relates directly to the *Experifaith* portrait. I heard the following story at a workshop several years ago, without attribution, and have unsuccessfully searched for its author. The following is my paraphrasing of the original.

Once upon a time, there was a glorious recipe for soup. The cook who created the recipe marveled at its uniqueness and soothing effects. He made copies of the recipe and encouraged other people to make the soup a part of their everyday lives. The recipe made its way around and was soon in every village, every farm, and every city. As the recipe spread, advocates were split into factions.

The largest group of soup devotees believed that everyone needed to *hear* about this wonderful recipe. They came together every night and read the recipe over and over again, wondering aloud how the soup would taste, speaking of how ecstatic life would be if they made the soup. They made copies of the recipe and distributed them to everyone they knew, encouraging people to read the recipe often. Some put together study groups and debated the wording of the recipe. This gave rise to different interpretations and eventually split the group into sects.

A smaller part of the group started *growing* the ingredients. They believed that agriculture was at the heart of the recipe because growing required character building, brought them closer to the earth, and made them humble to natural forces. With time, the group suffered defections, mainly because growing the ingredients was hard, tedious, and time-consuming.

A still smaller group made a momentous leap. They began measuring and eventually cooking the ingredients, but they did not eat the soup. Rather, they sat around every evening after a hard day of tilling the earth and delighted in the *aroma* of the soup. They felt that the others had missed the whole point of the recipe, which, to them, was to smell the aroma, so sweet and appealing, so vibrant and voluminous. And so they sat, night after night, engulfed in the fragrance.

The smallest group consisted of the precious few who *ate* the soup. This tiny group was the only one that realized that the true purpose of the recipe was to complete the cycle of reading, sharing, growing, smelling and then finally eating. Only they were full and sated.

EXPERIENTIAL INTERFAITH COMMUNICATIONS

"Theologians may quarrel, but the mystics of the world speak the same language."

Meister Eckhart (1260–1328)
German Theologian, Philosopher, and Mystic

History has taught us that when understanding and tolerance are fostered, people of different faiths can live together in harmony. Regrettably, history has also taught us the opposite, that such states of equilibrium can quickly degenerate and succumb to rhetoric of anger and fear, sometimes leading to violence and even war. A balance of mutual respect and tolerance needs to be maintained through good works. Interrelations need continual nurturing.

In that context, there are *four possible stages* of interfaith communications.

In our secular[15] Western society, the first stage, *tolerance,* is the most common form of interfaith relations. Tolerance is exemplified by the sentiment: "You are free to believe whatever you want, but please don't tell me about your faith or try to teach your theology to my kids."

Although this kind of tolerance may seem reluctant and lack understanding, it is far better than theocracy, where people are either considered second-class citizens if they do not submit themselves to the prevailing religious view or worse, are persecuted for their beliefs.

Ever since the Enlightenment era in the 17th and 18th Centuries — which, among other things, gave birth to the U.S. Constitution and the de facto motto *E Pluribus Unum* (out of the many, one) — interfaith tolerance has been sown into the fabric of Western society. The rules of one religion are not made into law for all citizens because of a simple social agreement. For you to believe what you want, you must allow me to do the same, even if we disagree. This kind of tolerance is periodically under attack and requires both maintenance and vigilance if it is to be sustained.

The second stage of interfaith relations is *openness.* "Maybe, just maybe, my truth isn't the only truth," is the sentiment that represents this worldview. While openness does not ask believers to change their religion or identity, it does ask them to acknowledge that *the truth* is a vast concept. Ultimate reality has many faces and all human systems

---

[15] The word *secular* here means a society for both those who want to be religious and those who don't want to be religious—*not* a non-religious society as some have suggested.

of thinking—note that even systems that are considered divine in nature entered their existence through a human filter, which makes them divinely inspired but human nonetheless—contain both truth and potential errors or oversights. By recognizing the vastness of truth, people enter into the mindset of humility.

At it's best, the stage of pluralistic openness leads to education about different religions and increased participation in interfaith services.

The third stage of interfaith relations is *experiential* in nature. It focuses on the communications that take place between spiritual practitioners of different faiths when they begin to compare their experiences. "How do you feel when you pray or meditate? What do the acts of service, tolerance, forgiveness, etc. do for your religious life? How does your spiritual life influence the way you act on a daily basis?"

This third stage epitomizes the kind of interaction that the *Experifaith* model promises to facilitate.

With experience as their guiding light, Christian monks and nuns could, for example, come together with Sufis and Yogis to pray and meditate, then discuss their *experiences* by talking about how silence and inner peace have changed their lives, instead of talking about the content of their prayers or focusing on theology.

Hindus, Christians, and Muslims, who tread the path of goodness, could come together and do good works. Doing good side by side would show them that they are not as different as previously thought and that their various beliefs can lead to similar outcomes.

The third stage mirrors a key insight that Swami

Vivekananda offered at the Parliament of World's Religions in 1893 when he said that "holiness, purity and charity" were not exclusive possessions of any one church and that all religious paths had produced "men and women of the most exalted character."

William James echoed that sentiment when he said that: "...the feelings on the one hand and the conduct on the other are almost always the same, for Stoic, Christian, and Buddhist saints are practically indistinguishable in their lives."[16]

Although rare, it is important to name the fourth stage of interfaith relations, which is *mystical union*, described to be more like an exchange of energy than a conventional process of communications. It takes place between mystics of different religions who have experienced either a personal communion with the divine or a direct revelation of their essence. The result is complete harmony.

Using *Experifaith* for Interfaith Dialogue

"I offer you peace. I offer you love. I offer you friendship. I see your beauty. I hear your need. I feel your feelings. My wisdom flows from the Highest Source. I salute that source within you. Let us work together for unity and love."

Mahatma Gandhi (1869–1948)
Civil Rights Leader and Nonviolent Visionary

When you make a decision to facilitate an experientially centered interfaith dialogue, your

---

[16] William James, *The Varieties of Religious Experience* (Longmans, Green & Co., 1902)

emphasis is placed on shared humanity. Ideally, the task is approached with a willingness to listen and be heard rather than to preach and be preached to. An ever-present spiritual undercurrent is allowed to pull participants into a deep discourse, and, throughout the process, everyone commits to conducting cordial interactions and resolving conflicts if they arise, working in harmony with others towards better understanding.

However, before you jump into the deep end and conduct such communications, you'll want to begin by discussing your *Experifaith* portrait with your family, friends, or faith group. Start locally and then, as you grow more comfortable with the process, expand your circle to include more people from diverse backgrounds.

When you are ready, groups of practitioners who want to engage in interfaith dialogue can be assembled in many ways, from announcing public meetings to co-operating with different faith communities.

Once a group is gathered, each participant will need an *Experifaith* portrait. The facilitator goes over the main tenets and asks participants to limit their discussions to how spiritual experiences have influenced three significant aspects of their lives, namely, their *feelings, thoughts,* and *actions.*

For example, a person can address his or her relationship with prayer by saying something like: "When I pray I *feel* [fill in the blank], I *think* [fill in the blank], and it encourages me to *act* [fill in the blank]."

The importance of this approach cannot be overstated. When a discussion revolves around the experiences of the person speaking—not around other people's behavior or theology in general[17] — it is much easier to relate to what they are saying.

The overall format is flexible. People can converse in pairs, engage in a roundtable format, or interact in other creative ways. You may want to introduce a talking stick or stone of some sort to ensure that the person speaking gets undivided attention.

Participants can start the dialogue by exploring both differences and similarities that come to light when portraits are compared, but after the initial comparison, conversations will probably take on a life of their own. The main thing is to encourage participants to get back on track when the discussion stops revolving around experiences.

At the end of the process, encourage everyone can share their insights with the entire group.

There are numerous benefits to this exercise.

On a personal level, participants are likely to see themselves in a new light. Even if they have already created an *Experifaith* portrait on their own, there is something magical that happens when people put their thoughts, feelings, and actions into words. Furthermore, actively taking the role of another, walking a mile in their shoes, has been shown to facilitate personal growth by increasing the number of perspectives a person can actively

---

[17] If participants wish to engage in conversations about religious stories and principles—which is completely natural and one reason why people participate in interfaith endeavors—remind them that as soon as they do that, as soon as they show interest in the narrative portion of another person's faith, they are exploring differences, not commonalities, and that is not what the *Experifaith* model was designed for.

entertain without necessarily making them their own, thusly decreasing self-centeredness.[18]

On a communal level, participants are building bridges and elevating understanding. By putting aside stories and disagreements and focusing on universal experiences, participants are automatically drawn closer to the people they are speaking with. Even when people seem to have nothing in common — their portraits being completely opposite — the mere willingness to listen is apt to have a positive effect.

It is important to note that people who only pay lip service to their faith or spiritual path will likely have a difficult time participating in this process.

An example would be the disparity between (1) a conversation where two people are both dedicated parents and (2) a conversation where one person is a parent while the other occasionally reads short articles about parenting. Without being rooted in experience, one part of the conversation is likely to end in mental gymnastics, with the non-parent expressing thoughts grounded in hearsay rather than firsthand knowledge.

With all that being said, when you decide to facilitate an interfaith discussion, approach the task with optimism. Be open-minded and expect the best. People who are willing to engage in these kinds of conversations usually want to expand their horizons.

Visit *www.experifaith.com* for resources.

---

[18] Ken Wilber, *Integral Psychology* (Shambhala, 2000)

THE PEARL NECKLACE OF
INTERSPIRITUALITY

"Interspirituality is essentially an agent of a universal mysticism and integral spirituality. We often walk the interspiritual or intermystical path in an intuitive attempt to reach a more complete truth. That final integration, a deep convergence, is an integral spirituality. Bringing together all the great systems of spiritual wisdom, practice, insight, reflection, experience, and science provides a truly integral understanding of spirituality in its practical application in our lives, regardless of our tradition."

Brother Wayne Teasdale (1945–2004)
Catholic monk and Interfaith Proponent

The conversation about humanity and religious diversity continues. Are we all completely different, like many social scientists believe, tribal in nature, prescribing to utterly distinctive beliefs? Or is there unity to be found between religions and faith traditions, like Ramakrishna, Aldous Huxley, Huston Smith, Ken Wilber, and others have asserted?

I choose to answer, both.

On the surface, we are all different. We ascribe to a variety of belief systems, attain our identity from various stories, get our customs from diverse cultures, and so on. And, rightly or wrongly, we generally define ourselves by these differences— there is no denying that. However, when we look beneath the surface, we discover certain universal elements.

It can be helpful to think of humanity like a pearl necklace. Each human being is a pearl with distinct characteristics, but underneath there is a string that ties us all together, invisible to the naked eye. Each one of us chooses which aspect to explore.

If we decide to explore differences, there are many. Some are easy to spot while others require data. A number of comparative fields in our society are continually looking for differences, and we shouldn't fault them for that—it's the stated focus of their profession.

Similarities, on the other hand, may not be as easy to find, and there are few fields of study dedicated to that endeavor. Nevertheless, if people choose to look for what human beings have in common, they will find that as well.

Experifaith is an excellent tool for such an enterprise. The experiential similarities unveiled in the model offer an opportunity to explore important fibers in the string the ties that pearl necklace of human spirituality together.

Final Thoughts

"I would like the church to be a place where the questions of people are honored rather than a place where we have all the answers. The church has to get out of propaganda. The future will involve us in more interfaith dialogue. We cannot say we have the only truth."

John Selby Spong (1931–)
Bishop of the Episcopal Church and Author

Once you are done reading this book, I encourage you to take a moment to reflect. What topics stood out? What did you agree with? Why? What did you disagree with? Why?

Digest the material and consider your next steps. Are you going to practice your faith or spiritual path at a deeper level and record your experiences? Are you going to fill in the portrait with your spouse or family and then discuss the implications? Are you going to bring the model into your place of worship and facilitate an intrafaith conversation? Or are you going to step out of your comfort zone and facilitate interfaith communications? Whatever you decide, remember that not doing is also doing.

On a final note, I'll be the first to admit that there is nothing new under the sun. Every song is a combination of existing notes, every book a combination of existing individual letters, and every recipe a combination of existing foods.

Experifaith follows the same blueprint. It's a recipe, a combination of existing ideas about faith and spirituality. I am in no way the first person to speak about duality, nonduality, and experiential similarities. Those ideas are thousands of years old.

Nonetheless, *Experifaith* is a unique recipe, both because of its approach and simplicity.

As I release the model into the world, I understand that it will likely take on a life of its own. I look forward to seeing how people use it to discover new aspects of their spiritual life, conduct interfaith dialogues, and find new uses that I haven't even dreamed of yet. My expectations are modest, but my hopes are high.

Irrespective of what happens, I can say that unveiling the *Experifaith* model has provided me with a long sought after sense of calm and coherence. I hope it does the same for you.

Blessings,

Gudjon Bergmann
www.experifaith.com

ABOUT THE AUTHOR

Gudjon Bergmann is an interfaith minister, author, and an experienced yoga and meditation teacher, who is committed to teaching interspiritual practices and improving interfaith relations.

He was born in Iceland in 1972, moved to America in 2010, and became a U.S. citizen in 2013.

Bergmann has spent much of his adult life studying spirituality and self-development and has authored more than twenty books, several of which were only published in his native Icelandic.

If you want to stay in touch, you can find him on several social media platforms.

Publications in English:

- *The Seven Human Needs*, 2006
- *Living in the Spirit of Yoga*, 2010
- *Create a Safe Space*, 2010
- *Know Thyself: Yoga Philosophy Made Accessible*, 2011

- *Yes! You Can Manage Stress*, 2011
- *Quit Smoking and Be Free*, 2011
- *The Author's Blueprint*, 2012
- *Balance: The Seven Human Needs Simplified*, 2013
- *The Presenter's Blueprint*, 2013
- *Empowerment Basics*, 2013
- *You Can't Have the Green Card*, 2014
- *Baby Steps to Meditation*, 2014
- *More Likely to Quote Star Wars than the Bible*, 2015
- *Trans-Rational Spirituality*, 2015
- *The Meditating Psychiatrist Who Tried to Kill Himself* (A Novel), 2016
- *Premature Holiness: Five Weeks at the Ashram* (A Novel), 2016
- *Experifaith: At the Heart of Every Religion*, 2017

Made in the USA
Lexington, KY
29 May 2017